THE END
OF THE WILD

THE END
OF THE WILD

Stephen M. Meyer

BOSTON REVIEW Somerville, Mass.

THE MIT PRESS Cambridge, Mass. London, England

MIT Press books may be purchased at special quantity
discounts for business or sales promotional use. For
information, please e-mail special_sales@mitpress.mit.edu or
write to Special Sales Department, The MIT Press,
55 Hayward Street, Cambridge, MA 02142.

This book was set in Adobe Garamond by *Boston Review*
and was printed and bound in the United States of America.

Designed by Joshua J. Friedman

Library of Congress Cataloging-in-Publication Data
Meyer, Stephen M.
    The end of the wild / Stephen M. Meyer.
        p.   cm. — (Boston Review books)
    Includes bibliographical references.
    ISBN-13: 978-0-262-13473-6 (hardcover : alk. paper)
    ISBN-10: 0-262-13473-X (hardcover : alk. paper)
    1. Biodiversity conservation. I. Title.
QH75.M478 2006
333.95—dc22   2006021914

10   9   8   7   6   5   4   3   2   1

For Seth and Debbie

CONTENTS

THE END
OF THE WILD

1

FOR THE PAST SEVERAL BILLION YEARS evolution on Earth has been driven by small-scale incremental forces, such as sexual selection, punctuated by cosmic-scale disruptions—plate tectonics, planetary geochemistry, global climate shifts, and even extraterrestrial asteroids. Sometime in the last century that changed. Today the guiding hand of natural selection is unmistakably human, with potentially Earth-shaking consequences.

The fossil record and contemporary field studies suggest that the average rate of extinction over the past hundred million years has hovered at several species per year. Today the extinction rate surpasses 3,000 species per year and is accelerating rapidly; it may soon reach the tens of thousands. In contrast, new species are appearing at a rate of less than one per year.

Over the next 100 years or so as many as half of the Earth's species, representing a quarter of the planet's genetic stock, will functionally if not completely disappear. The land and the oceans will continue to teem with life, but it will be a peculiarly homogenized assemblage of organisms unnaturally selected for their compatibility with one fundamental force: us. Nothing—not national or international laws, global bioreserves, local sustainability schemes, or even "wildlands" fantasies—can change the current course. The broad path for biological evolution is now set for the next several million years. And in this sense the extinction crisis—the race to save the composition, structure, and organization of biodiversity as it exists today—is over, and we have lost.

2

THIS IS NOT THE WIDE-EYED PROPHECY of radical Earth First! activists or the doom-and-gloom tale of corporate environmentalists trying to boost fundraising. It is the story that lurks behind a growing mountain of scientific papers published in prestigious scientific journals such as *Nature*, *Science*, and the *Proceedings of the National Academy of Sciences* over the past decade.

Our sense of the wild is perhaps best captured in the opening paragraphs of the U.S. Wilderness Act of 1964, which defines "wilderness" as follows:

an area where the earth and its community of life are untrammeled by man, where man himself is a visitor who does not remain … retaining its primeval character and influence, without permanent improvements or human habitation, which is protected and managed so as to preserve its natural conditions and which generally appears to have been affected primarily by the forces of nature, with the imprint of man's work substantially unnoticeable.

Fundamental is the notion of a landscape where the handprint of humanity is invisible—and specifically where the forces of natural selection smother those of human selection. The problem is that there is virtually no place left on Earth that fits this definition. From the most remote corners of the frozen Arctic to the darkest interiors of the Amazon's tropical rainforests, the impact of humanity now drives biological systems. What separates the Brazilian rain-forest from New York's Adirondack Forest Preserve from Manhattan's Central Park is only a matter of degree.

Through our extraordinary capacity to modify the world around us, we human beings are creating a three-tiered hierarchy of life. The great irony here is that this anthropogenic transformation of the biosphere springs as much from our deliberate efforts to protect and manage the life around us as from our wanton disregard for the natural environment.

At one extreme we are making the planet especially hospitable for the *weedy species*: plants, animals, and other organisms that thrive in continually disturbed, human-dominated environments. The term is not pejorative but descriptive. Weedy organisms are adaptive generalists—species that flourish in a variety of ecological settings, switch easily between food types, and breed prolifically. More significantly, many have their needs met more completely and efficiently by humans than by Mother Nature. In the United States, for example, one can find five times as many raccoons (*Procyon lotor*) per square mile in suburban settings than in corresponding natural populations in the wild. Aquatic plants such as Eurasian watermilfoil (*Myriophyllum spicatum*) and hydrilla (*Hydrilla verticillata*), growing in streams, rivers, ponds, and lakes enriched by the runoff from farms, suburban development, and sewage treatment facilities, reach densities never encountered in natural settings.

From dandelions to coyotes, weedy species will enjoy expanding populations, spatial distribution, ecological dominance, and opportunities for further speciation far into the future. Some weedy species have become so comfortable living among us that we now consider many of them to be pests, requiring active control measures: the common (Norway) rat (*Rattus norvegicus*) and the white-tailed deer (*Odocoileus virginianus*) come immediately to mind.

Living on the margins in ever-decreasing numbers and contracting spatial distribution are *relic species*. Relic species do not thrive in human-dominated environments—which now nearly cover the planet. Some relic species have always been rare, persisting in small, isolated populations, often in extreme or remote environments. Having adapted to these specialized conditions, they have survived largely through benign neglect, inhabiting places that humans traditionally did not bother to go.

But little on Earth is remote anymore, and accelerating human pressures on the landscape threaten to overrun even specialized habitats. When the Nature Conservancy in 2004 undertook a five-week expedition into four Borneo karst systems, they quickly discovered a number of insect and plant species previously unknown to science as well as cataloguing 124 species of bird and 34 species of bats. They also discovered that logging and mining activity was moving rapidly into the area. The very specialization that allows natural relics to live in these habitats makes it impossible for them to disperse across the landscape to escape threats. Instead they perish—many before they are even discovered.

Hundreds of thousands of formerly well-established organisms are now spilling into the ranks of the relics. Unlike natural relics, most of them are not capable of lingering on the edges of existence. These forced relics hang on in the wild either as ecologically marginalized populations or as carefully managed boutique populations, all the while facing the threat of extinction as suitable habitat shrinks. Progressively reduced and isolated relics such as the African elephant (*Loxodonta africana*) and the giant panda (*Ailoropoda melanoleuca*) have already become genetic dead ends. To survive outside of zoos, relics will require our permanent and direct management, including captive breeding and continuous restocking. It is through such intervention that the Sumatran rhinoceros (*Dicerorhinus sumatrensis*), the California condor (*Gymnogyps californianus*), and virtually all of Hawaii's endemic plants continue to exist in the wild at all—albeit as living trophies.

But most relics will not be fortunate enough to be the focus of special conservation programs. And of those that do attract such attention, many will not respond. These are the *ghost species*—organisms that will not survive on a planet with billions of people, because of their abilities and our choices. They are ghosts because while they may seem plentiful today and may in fact persist for decades, their extinction is certain, apart from a few specimens in zoos or laboratory-archived DNA samples.

Some ghost species, such as the East Asian giant soft-shell turtle (extirpated except for one left in the wild) and the dusky seaside sparrow (extinct), are incapable of adapting their highly specialized needs rapidly enough to keep up with human pressures. Some of these we ignore. Others we intentionally try to eradicate. Although they are protected today (and for now), gray wolves and black-tailed prairie dogs in North America were once hunted for extermination as part of federal and state animal-control programs (unofficially, they still are). In Africa, the lion (*Panthera leo*) population has plunged from over 200,000 in 1980 to under 20,000 today because of preemptive eradication by livestock herders who wish to reduce predation threats.

Other ghosts we simply consume beyond their capacity to successfully reproduce and persist in the wild—for food, for commercial products, or as pets. Recent studies suggest that we have eliminated 90 percent of the stocks of large predatory fish, such as tuna and swordfish, in the world's oceans. And while 10,000 tigers live as pets in the United States, fewer than 7,000 live in the wild throughout the world!

A great many of the plants and animals we perceive as healthy and plentiful today are in fact relics or ghosts. This seeming contradiction is explained by the fact that species loss is not a simple linear process. Many decades can pass between the start of the decline and the observable collapse of a population structure, especially where moderate-to-long-lived life forms are involved. Conservation biologists use the term "extinction debt" to describe this gap between appearance and reality. In the past century we have accumulated a vast extinction debt that will be paid in the century ahead. The number of plants and animals we discover to be threatened will spiral as the extinction debt comes due.

Thus, over the next hundred years, perhaps half of the Earth's species are destined to become relics or ghosts in the wild, while weedy species will constitute an ever-growing proportion of the plants and animals around us. By virtue of their compatibility with us, weedy species can follow us around the planet, filling in habitat vacated by relics and ghosts and creating additional vacancies through predation and parasitism. More and more we will encounter on every continent remarkably similar, if not the very same, species of plants, insects, mammals, birds, and other organisms organized in similar and simple communities. Ecosystems will experience a dumbing down as built-in redundancies are eliminated. The web of life will become the strand of life.

3

ALTHOUGH WE HAVE BEEN AWARE OF species losses for decades, only recently has it become apparent that the biotic world as we have known it is collapsing. The causes, varied and complex, fall into three broad disturbance categories: landscape transformation, geochemical modification (pollution), and biotic consumption and manipulation. Each reflects some aspect of human manipulation of the environment, as these examples from the news illustrate:

¶ New housing developments in Scotland will destroy critical habitat for Britain's threatened red squirrel (*Sciurus vulgaris*), which has disappeared from most of its former range.

¶ Logging and agricultural development have reduced the distribution of Chile's famed national tree—the monkey puzzle tree (*Araucaria araucana*)—to three small areas of the country, where it is vulnerable to fire and illegal logging.

¶ A new dam in Belize will flood vital habitat for rare species of jaguars, macaws, and crocodiles in a valley linking to wildlife preserves.

¶ Biologically active quantities of common over-the-counter and prescription drugs (e.g., Prozac) are ubiquitous in European and North American urban and suburban waste waters, where discharge to streams and rivers wreaks havoc on the endocrine systems of aquatic animals.

❡ Polar bears endure body concentrations of PCB and other industrial toxins hundreds of times higher than those of animals living where the pollutants are emitted, thousands of miles away.

❡ Eighty percent of Caribbean corals have died off in the past two decades from diseases fueled by pollution from municipal waste-water treatment plants and agricultural runoff flooding into coastal waters.

❡ Demand for "bush meat" in Africa (which sells for 30 percent of the price of farmed meat) is now outstripping supply, seriously depleting wildlife in general and great apes in particular. Meanwhile, the international trade in bush meat and animal parts is growing rapidly, fetching prices many times those in domestic markets.

❡ During the past two years half of the world's remaining Sumatran tigers (*Panthera tigris sumatrae*) were wiped out by trophy hunters, leaving fewer than 300 animals in the wild and ensuring the extirpation of the species.

¶ Collecting freshwater and marine fish for the aquarium trade reduces wild populations of targeted species by 75 percent in commercial collection areas.

¶ Cheatgrass, introduced into North America around 1900, has displaced native vegetation across broad areas of rangeland in the West, devastating the local ecology. A prolific annual of low nutritive value, cheatgrass dries up early in the season, fueling range fires that wipe out native plants and leave little food or shelter for wildlife.

¶ Native aquatic food webs in South America are being destroyed by the introduction of the North American bullfrog (*Rana catesbeiana*)—a voracious predator.

When these factors—development, agriculture, resource consumption, pollution, and alien species—are considered separately, the problems seems manageable. Sprawl can be countered by smart growth. The demand for agricultural land and high-intensity farming can be dampened through dietary changes. The overconsumption of natural resources through logging, hunting, fishing, and the exotic pet trade can be reduced through education, regulation, and policing. And the proliferation of alien species can be stopped through better laws and inspections.

But this is a gross simplification. The power of human selection comes from its multiplicative nature. Small effects of one type are magnified by small effects of others. Consider the plight of a simple, undemanding, and modestly adaptable creature:

the California tiger salamander (*Ambystoma californiense*). These amphibians live most of the year underground in upland fields and woodlands. Each winter they migrate thousands of feet to their natal breeding pools to find mates and lay eggs. After several weeks of carousing they return to their burrows.

The key to the breeding success of these salamanders is the ephemeral nature of the pools. For six months of the year they exist as dry depressions. Then, as heavy spring rains flood the region, the shallow basins fill with water, creating vernal pools that cannot support the local fish populations. Thus, the salamanders' eggs are relatively safe from predation. As the eggs hatch, the larvae find themselves immersed in a bath of food: the water is bursting with millions of planktonic organisms. The salamander larvae grow rapidly—and they need to, because with the rains gone the pools dry up quickly, and unless the juvenile salamanders mature and move out into the surrounding terrain they will die. And so it has been for millions of years.

But not anymore. Today the California tiger salamander is disappearing. First, the upland habitat where it lives is prime real estate for residential, commercial, and agricultural development. Between 50 and 75 percent of its native habitat has already been lost, and more than 100 development projects are pending in the remaining areas. Woodlands are cut down and fields plowed up to make room for houses, lawns, schools, shopping centers, and roadways. Many vernal pools are simply filled.

Where pools are spared bulldozing they are pressed into service as roadside storm basins to collect runoff from lawns, roads, and driveways—water saturated with fertilizers, herbicides, pesticides, and heavy metals. The nitrogen and phosphorus stimulate massive algal blooms that drive oxygen levels in the pools down to deadly levels, suffocating a large proportion of the animals. The herbicides and pesticides kill many juveniles and, in lower doses, alter metabolic chemistry in ways that bizarrely change sexual development, immune function, and even limb development.

Even setting aside local sources of contamination, the water in the pools is increasingly laden with a cocktail of toxic compounds that are not used locally. Blowing in from industrial and agricultural sites many hundreds of miles away, these endocrine-disrupting compounds significantly reduce breeding success and foster grotesque developmental abnormalities.

Then there is the army of alien species—bullfrogs, crayfish, and other predators—that have been introduced intentionally into the landscape. These voracious hunters consume huge numbers of salamander larvae and juveniles. In some instances, non-native salamanders (former pets) have been released into local pools, reducing breeding success and posing the risk of hybridization. And fish are frequently added to the temporary pools to devour mosquitoes during the wet season. While this makes life more comfortable for nearby human inhabitants, it exhausts the young salamanders' food supply.

But the assault does not end there. The regularity of spring rains is being replaced by recurrent three- and four-year droughts. Several generations of tiger salamanders therefore never emerge to replace the animals lost to natural and unnatural causes. In the past, tiger salamanders persisted despite climate variations by wandering through networks of wetlands until they chanced upon new vernal pools and restarted the population. But that is no longer possible because the matrix of connecting wetlands has been eliminated, and habitat fragmentation makes the chance encounter with a car tire orders of magnitude more likely than an encounter with either a suitable mate or a suitable habitat.

Finally, where isolated populations of tiger salamanders have survived despite the odds, they have become a target of the pet trade. Children are paid 25 cents per salamander to collect these highly prized animals, which are then sold for $15 apiece in U.S. pet shops and for more than $200 overseas. In fact the global trade in "exotics" such as tiger salamanders is growing explosively, especially for reptiles and amphibians. Probably one in a thousand salamanders survives the commerce, and of those perhaps one in a thousand survives a few years in captivity.

This story is neither exaggerated nor unusual. It is, in fact, the rule. One could tell similar stories of the red-crowned crane (*Grus japonensis*), the leatherback sea turtle (*Dermochelys coriacea*), the Lesothan succulent *Aloe polyphylla*, and most other species in decline. Relic species generally face an overwhelming web of threats that are impossible to disentangle.

Further complicating the picture are two human-caused meta-disturbances: global climate change and economic globalization. Climate change will make many historically reliable habitats inhospitable. Entire biotic communities will be evicted: coastal wetlands will be permanently submerged, cloud forests will dry out, some dry savannas will become lush while others become deserts. During the past decade in South America, for example, many dozens of species of frogs have disappeared forever. They were exterminated by a combination of evaporating cloud cover and a deadly fungus whose explosive growth was fueled by the warming of the cloud-forest regions—a direct consequence of climate change.

Although the types of climate shifts we can expect over the next century are within the experiential history of most species that have survived the last two million years, their survival was insured to a large extent by dispersal across the landscape. But today only weedy species have the broad distribution, adaptability, and migratory capacity to reestablish thriving populations in new habitats, which now and in the future will invariably be human-disturbed areas. For the rest, there is either no place to go because acceptable habitat has been reduced to a few isolated patches in a sea of human development, or no way for them to get to more suitable locations because the barriers presented by interposed cities, roadways, subdivisions, shopping centers, industrial parks, and farms are too great to overcome. Some preliminary research suggests that this simple inability to disperse in the wake of minimum projected climate change may double the rate at which species become relics and ghosts.

Economic globalization exacerbates the species-loss problem in several ways. Globalization increases the demand for natural resources in remote and undeveloped regions. In locations previously occupied by subsistence villages, labor towns spring up to support foreign timber and mining operations. As foreign capital flows into undeveloped regions it inflates the price paid for local goods, thereby increasing incentives for overexploitation to feed the lucrative export market. Timber from the Malaysian and Indonesian rainforests bought and paid for by Japanese firms brings a much higher return than the same lumber sold in local markets. More than 80 percent of these rainforests have now been logged, slicing the orangutan population to less than ten percent of what it was decades ago. In Brazil the greatest single threat to the Amazon rainforests is beef production headed for the global market, which has increased sixfold since 1999.

Furthermore, the flow of money into less-developed regions spurs local economic demands—for development, services, and advanced commodities. Pressures on the local landscape increase proportionately.

The booming trade of the globalized economy also accelerates the pace of alien species being transported around the planet—intentionally and unintentionally. Breaking down economic barriers effectively breaks down geographic, ecological, and biotic barriers as vast numbers of plants and animals are shipped worldwide to support the pet and horticultural trades. (As a reference point, 25 percent of the vascular plants in the United States today are alien species.) The prickly-pear cactus (*Opuntia stricta*) was deliberately imported into Australia in the 1920s as a natural fencing material. Today it is considered that continent's worst weed, covering over 95,000 square miles in six feet of impenetrable cactus. Although only about five percent of these aliens take hold and flourish in their new environs, five percent of an exploding number is still quite large.

Unintended introductions of alien plants, animals, and other organisms are all the more threatening since authorities make no attempt to screen out truly harmful organisms. Alien pests, parasites, and predators take an increasingly high toll on native ecosystems. As ships and planes shuttle between continents carrying unprecedented volumes of cargo, they cart with them a growing number of stowaways. The Asian long-horn beetle (*Anoplophora glabripennis*), for example, invaded the United States in 1996 encased in wood crates from China or Korea. Spreading through New York and Chicago, they decimated local trees, especially maples. Since then, adult beetles have been intercepted at 17 U.S. ports.

Thus, climate change and economic globalization are powerful agents of human selection that amplify and make irreversible the familiar, localized human disturbances that undermine biodiversity.

4

As our awareness of the extinction crisis has grown, we have taken some ameliorative actions. In the United States we have imposed rules upon ourselves to try to halt the loss. The Endangered Species Act prohibits the taking, harm, or harassment of some 1,300 plants and animals designated by the U.S. Fish and Wildlife Service. Some critical habitats of these species have also been protected. And 44 of the 50 states have some form of state-level endangered species act through which they try to protect locally threatened species.

Since the early 1990s the European Union has had its Habitat Directive, which makes it illegal to kill or harm about 700 protected species or to disrupt 168 specially designated habitats. Approaching the problem from a different angle is the Convention on the International Trade of Endangered Species, or CITES, which, as the name implies, is an attempt by the international community—presently over 150 countries—to limit the global trade in threatened species. About 30,000 plants and animals are on the CITES list. Thousands of species are added annually.

Meanwhile, acting individually and through international conventions, nations have attempted to set aside biologically valuable landscapes and ocean areas as wildlife refuges and bioreserves. More than ten percent of the Earth has now been pledged or protected. The Parsa Reserve in Nepal covers about 500 square kilometers and offers sanctuary to a range of creatures, including 300 species of birds. The Northwestern Hawaiian Islands Coral Reef Ecosystem Reserve, encompassing over 400,000 square kilometers of ocean, protects about 70 percent of the coral reef ecosystems in the United States. Over 7,000 marine species are associated with this area, of which 25 percent are found nowhere else on the planet.

Recognizing that governments have limited political and fiscal resources and that biodiversity is a problem that transcends national borders, nongovernmental organizations have moved to impede the flow of species loss by assisting in land protection, policy enforcement, public education, litigation, and policy advocacy. The Nature Conservancy claims to have helped to preserve more than 117 million acres of wildlife habitat over the past 50-plus years. In the United States the Center for Biological Diversity, Defenders of Wildlife, and others use the courts to force recalcitrant government agencies to implement and enforce existing conservation laws and regulations.

A casual reading of the news would suggest these efforts are paying off:

¶ In 1939 the number of whooping cranes (*Grus americana*) in the United States had declined to 18. Thanks to captive breeding, today there are over 300 whooping cranes, with 180 living in the wild. In an astounding effort, humans piloting ultralight aircraft taught a novice flock how to migrate from Florida to Wisconsin.

¶ The population of Puerto Rican crested toads (*Peltophryne lemur*) has tripled to 300 over the past 25 years thanks to captive breeding in U.S. zoos and restocking in the wild.

❡ A recent survey of tigers in India's Sunderbans Forest suggests that the preserve's population is stable and may even reflect an increase in cubs.

❡ The last remaining patch of Kneeland prairie penny-cress (*Thlaspi californicum*), found in only one California county, will be saved with a ten-year, $300,000 conservation effort.

Perhaps if we dedicated a few billion dollars more, increased cooperative efforts among governments, expanded the system of bioreserves, cultivated sustainable economics among local communities, and reduce human consumption habits we could save the Earth's biota.

Unfortunately, such efforts are far too little and far, far too late. In fact these and similar apparent success stories reflect a much more insidious process that is reshaping the living Earth. Our most common tools for preserving biodiversity—prohibitory laws and regulations, bioreserves, and sustainable-development programs—are themselves powerful engines of human selection, tweaking (for our pleasure) but not fundamentally altering the outcome: massive species loss with the attendant disappearance of the wild.

PROHIBITORY REGULATION Virtually by definition all regulatory efforts at species protection and recovery are focused on relics and (unknowingly) ghosts, which have no chance of *true* recovery. Occasionally there are extraordinary exceptions, such as the American alligator, which having been almost extirpated is once again abundant. But the very few alleged successes are nothing more than manifestations of the growing dominance of human selection in evolution.

The very notion that we could regulate ourselves out of the extinction crisis—that government could force the wild to remain wild—is based on a fundamentally false premise: that the causes of species extinction are finite and reducible and the number of true threatened species reasonably limited. When the Endangered Species Act was recrafted in the early 1970s, wildlife experts naively believed that at most a few hundred species would require protection. Today the list of domestic endangered species tops 1,300, and the number would be almost 5,000 if politics did not prevent it. (Species may be placed on the list only after a biological review by the U.S. Fish and

Wildlife Service. Practically all such reviews are today initiated by petitions from environmental groups. The Bush administration has halted these reviews, claiming it has run out of money.)

The great irony is that the Endangered Species Act itself is the institutionalization of human-driven evolution. We decide which species get on the list for protection and which are kept off. We decide the recovery goals: how many of a given plant or animal should be allowed to persist, in how many populations and in which locations. The gray-wolf recovery plan for the northern Rockies stipulated 30 breeding pairs and a population of about 300 animals, confined to carefully delineated areas in a few designated states. Animals that do not obey the rules may be killed in the name of protecting local cattle ranching.

Of the 1,274 species listed under the Endangered Species Act some 599 are plants. Yet the U.S. Fish and Wildlife Service spends less than five percent of what it spends on animals on plants. And its goals are limited to restoring plant populations where they are presently growing as relics and ghosts, not to restoring their former range.

We decide which habitats of listed species are critical and which expendable. In 2003, for example, the U.S. Fish and Wildlife Service estimated that 1.1 million acres potentially qualified as critical habitat for the California tiger salamander. By the spring of 2005 that number had been cut to 382,000 acres. Why? Because restricting the other 700,000 acres would hinder housing construction. Just a few months later, in August of 2005, the Fish and Wildlife Service cut the critical habitat to 199,000 acres. Why? More housing construction. Thus, one of the primary mechanisms behind the destruction of the tiger salamander—landscape development—became the primary criterion by which land was excluded from habitat protection.

Similarly, International Whaling Commission rules, CITES, and other international conventions convert human values into biotic structure; they are not regimes designed for ecological restoration. How many minke whales are sufficient to allow hunting? How many zoo requests for gorillas should be honored? Fundamentally, the determination of which species make it onto these protection lists is more about aesthetics and economics than ecology and biology. Pandas get lots of attention and support; the many thousands of disappearing aquatic invertebrates do not.

Although legal prohibitions and strict enforcement can preserve some relic species at the margins and temporarily forestall the extinction of ghost species, they cannot prevent or even slow the end of the wild. Regulation does little more than transform nature into a product of the human imagination—like a Disney cartoon.

REFUGES AND PRESERVES Biologists and ecologists have long recognized the limitations of species-specific preservation and have lobbied instead for the creation of protected areas that would shield ecosystems and all the plants and animals within. The idea behind refuges and bioreserves is to wall off the wild from the harmful disturbances of humanity. Set aside 20,000 acres, limit human activity, and allow nature to proceed unhindered in its special space.

And for a while this appears to work. But this too is largely an illusion. The refuges and bioreserves we set aside are no more than our paltry conception of an ecosystem, and a good number the species within their boundaries are relics and ghosts—part of the extinction debt—all the while in decline. A recent analysis found that the entire U.S. wildlife refuge system can, at best, assist in the meaningful conservation of about 20 percent of listed animal species (the list itself being only a fraction of the total species in trouble).

As presently managed, bioreserves are the proverbial barrel in which fish are more easily shot: three quarters of the deaths of large carnivores in bioreserves are caused by people. The failures of this approach have been obvious for while, especially to those with first-hand experience. In particular, direct and indirect human encroachment into bioreserves is relentless and, with ever-expanding populations in the developing world, unavoidable. The Montes Azules Bioreserve encompasses 820,000 acres of rainforest—the last rainforest in North America. Half of Mexico's bird species and over 100 mammal species live there; ten percent of Mexico's fresh water originates there. Yet in the past 30 years illegal logging and agricultural development has consumed a quarter of the forest. In 20 years the bioreserve will be completely gone. In Africa and Asia, bioreserves have become the preferred hunting grounds for poachers and bush-meat traders: it is, after all, where the animals are.

Bioreserves as currently designed will always be too small and too isolated from each other to accomplish their stated goal of preserving the wild as it is today. Embedded in a matrix of human habitation—cities, towns, farms, mining and logging operations—they cannot be insulated from broader human disturbances in the region, even if their own boundaries remain inviolate. The ecosystems they encompass are already in serious trouble.

Consider one of the world's favorite ecotourist destinations: the Monteverde Cloud Forest Preserve. This ecologically significant area covers more than 30,000 acres and hosts more than 2,500 plant species, 100 mammalian species, 400 bird species, 120 reptilian and amphibian species, and thousands of insects. The problem is that the cloud forest appears to be drying out. Deforestation is the apparent cause, but not from logging in the preserve. Rather, the clearing of lowland areas outside the preserve for agriculture is causing changes in the local patterns of fog and mist formation, thereby altering cloud formation up in the preserve. Thus, despite strong protections within its boundaries, the cloud forest may soon lack its defining feature: clouds. And the multitude of species that depend on that moisture will go the way of the extinct golden toad.

This weakness in the call for specific ecosystem preservation becomes all the more apparent in the context of climate change. The creation of a network of isolated, independent bioreserves assumes that the global environment—in particular the global climate—is relatively static. For the past 11,000 years this would have been a fair assumption. But things have changed. Climate models project far cooler and wetter weather during the critical winter months in what are now the most important Monarch-butterfly wintering grounds in Mexico, the

Monarch Butterfly Bioreserve, which will become unlivable to the insects over the next few decades. Similar problems confront many of Europe's protected birds.

Lastly, by concentrating species within a limited geographic area, bioreserves increase the vulnerability of relic species to catastrophic, unrecoverable losses from natural disasters, epizootic diseases, war, and so on. During the summer of 2003, for example, fires in Brazil's two refuges that are home to the Brazilian Merganser duck (*Mergus octosetaceus*) wiped out 70 percent of one of the 53,000-square-kilometer parks while decimating large parts of the other, which may lead to the creature's extinction. Only 250 existed *before* the fire.

For this reason, some scientists have actually suggested transplanting African megafauna—elephants and cheetahs, for example—to newly created wildlife reserves in North America. While from a species-centric perspective this may seem to make sense, from an ecological and evolutionary perspective it makes no sense at all. Rescuing charismatic megafauna may make us feel better, but there is no evidence to suggest that there are niches in North American ecosystems waiting to be filled by these alien species.

On the other hand, one can certainly imagine how the movement of significant numbers of exotic species to new continents could wreak havoc with the receiving ecosystems. This is human selection in capital letters.

Ultimately, the transformation of wilderness into a patchwork of static bioreserves is just another form of human selection—the antithesis of the wild.

SUSTAINABLE COMMUNITIES Much has been said about sustainable communities as a social approach to easing the extinction crisis. Sustainability has been something of a crusade for the UN, various international agencies, and many nongovernmental environmental organizations. The argument goes that if local communities could learn to live within the carrying capacity of their environs, the pressures on terrestrial and marine ecosystems would be eased. And of course this is true.

But in the context of the extinction crisis, sustainable development is an anthropocentric resource-use policy, not an ecological model. Consumptive demand measured against resource supply, not ecosystem function, determines the limit of sustainability. What is the maximum amount of mahogany, or tuna, or leopard pelts that can be harvested and still allow projected human demand for the product to be met for the foreseeable future? The demands of the ecosystem are not truly part of the equation.

In addition, for sustainable development to have an impact on conservation it must be tied directly to local demand, where the costs of overexploitation are borne by those who benefit from it. This makes sustainable economic programs a moving target because communities grow. As medical services and standards of living improve, the size of a community, its economic aspirations, and its demands for resources grow. What was sustainable for a Kenyan village in 2000 will not be sustainable in 2020. The gradual collapse of Africa's wildlife populations in the face of the bush-meat trade is just one example.

Moreover, if there was ever a hope for this strategy, globalization destroyed it. Consider what might be regarded as an exemplar of sustainable development: Brazil-nut harvesting in the Amazon. Originally the idea was to protect the rainforest by creating a local economy based on the collection and sale of Brazil nuts. And initially it succeeded. But today, residents of the Brazilian Amazon harvest more than 45,000 tons of nuts from the forest floor each year, yielding some $43 million in global trade. So many nuts are harvested that few seedlings are taking root. As aging Brazil-nut trees die off, they will not be replaced. Global demand for this environmentally friendly, sustainable crop drives the harvest and has made it unsustainable in the long term.

Similarly, the depletion of global fish stocks shows the basic flaw in the sustainability strategy. Local fishermen selling to local people are not the problem. The problem is the rise of global markets. Gross disparities in wealth between those who supply low-wage labor and those who demand high-wage developed societies ensure that sustainability will always be a function of maximum bearable price, not ecological balance.

Even so-called low-impact activities that many feel promote biodiversity, such as ecotourism, fail the test. As ecotourism expands, visitors unwittingly introduce alien species into formerly safe habitats. As tourists clamor for more-advanced infrastructure, sites compete for customers, the exposure to wealth stokes local aspirations for economic development, and the human impact on the landscape grows. Economics trumps ecology.

The notion of sustainable communities, then, is not about the wild. It is about long-term economic efficiency and the wise use of natural resources.

WILDLANDS The wildlands concept is fantastic—wonderful and unreal. This idea, advocated by those in the deep-ecology movement, has two main components. First, human communities within nations would be resettled into tightly drawn sustainable enclaves. In the United States, for example, huge areas of former ecological significance such as Florida and the Rocky Mountains would be depopulated and restored to a natural state. About 50 percent of the United States would be converted into an expansive set of connected wildlands, surrounded by extensive buffers. Human access to this half of the country would be prohibited. Similar wildlands could be created on every continent.

Second, extensive social engineering would be necessary to alter land use and consumption patterns. The goal would be to reduce the ecological footprint of humanity so that much of the planet could be free from human exploitation.

In theory this strategy could reduce the slide of ghosts and relics into oblivion if it could be implemented immediately and universally. For example, wildlands could help species, populations, and natural communities to adapt to climate change. As an ecologically centered strategy it is most likely the only approach that could truly reduce the scale of the biotic collapse that is already underway.

Yet the notion that upwards of seven billion people could bend their needs to nature's is hard to accept. With the right social framework we might have been able to do it modestly in 1307, but not in 2007 and certainly not in 2107. Global society is moving rapidly and inexorably in the opposite direction.

To be fair, advocates of wildlands acknowledge that, owing to enormous social, political, and economic hurdles, their vision would be at minimum a 100-year undertaking. The problem, of course, is that by then the end of the wild will already be well at hand.

GENETIC ENGINEERING Some suggest that genetic engineering can end the cascade of species loss. Why can't we store DNA and, once the technology matures, bring all the species back and release them into the wild?

This kind of *Jurassic Park* thinking ignores the fact that all of the factors that contributed to species loss in the wild will remain in place and probably be even more powerful. If 95 percent of desert-tortoise habitat has been developed and its primary diet of herbs, grasses, and desert flowers is no longer available in 2004, exactly where will our reengineered tortoises live in 2030? At best they could exist as genetic relics in a zoo.

The wild will cease to exist even if we can individually manufacture each of its constituent parts.

5

IF WE ARE UNALTERABLY MOVING TO a world in which perhaps half of existing species will be relics or ghosts—if in this respect the current extinction crisis is truly over—why should we continue to do anything to protect and manage biodiversity? Why not rescind national and international laws protecting endangered species, eliminate bioreserves, and let the unfettered market determine how and where we consume natural resources? By taking refuge in the serendipitous elements of human selection in setting the course of biotic development and evolution we could bulldoze, pave, or grass over the planet in the pursuit of human progress guilt-free. For example, the Puerto Rican coqui (*Eleutherodactylus coqui*), a tree frog, is under increasing pressure from development and pollution at home, where it may soon be extirpated. But in Hawaii, where it was illegally introduced, it thrives in the resort and residential communities heavily planted with exotic, alien tropical species. Here human selection seems to have solved the human problem: the coqui will live on. Why not let human selection, operating through benign neglect, allow the weedy species to define the new wild?

The answer is simple: the end of the wild as described so far is not the worst possible outcome. Although the marginal utility of national and international regulation, work by NGOs, and the creation and management of bioreserves has already reached the point of little additional positive return—these efforts cannot prevent the end of the wild—the multiplicative aspect of human selection means that doing less could produce an end of a far more disastrous nature.

The benign-neglect approach would over the long term effectively bifurcate the Earth's biota into weedy species and ghost species. Virtually all the organisms that would have become relics—some of which might have persisted with a fairly stable presence—would instead become ghosts, pauperizing natural communities and greatly multiplying the extinction debt. Weedy species would be elevated to keystone status in every ecosystem and community. (A keystone species is one that has a disproportionately large impact on ecosystem processes such as biomass production, energy transfer, and nutrient cycling.) Meanwhile, the time scale for the compounded effects of human selection could contract to decades rather than more than a century, causing ecosystems to collapse rather than degrade.

Nor would this human-selected biosphere emerging from benign neglect necessarily be a human-friendly one. Without direct management many wild species that we view as key natural resources, such as timber trees and marine fish, would be consumed out of functional existence. Although economists tell us that such a thing is impossible, in truth the invisible hand of the market is all too invisible when it comes to the exploitation of natural commodities. The multiple collapses of once bountiful Atlantic and Pacific fisheries—which are now regulated, albeit poorly—represent just a taste of what would happen without any controls in place. (The North Atlantic, for example, holds less than 20 percent of the fish it held in 1900.) The destructive effects would rebound through the economies of every continent as once plentiful natural resources became relics and ghosts.

Across entire hemispheres certain types of ecosystems and biotic communities, such as mangrove swamps and sea-grass meadows, might completely disappear as functional entities. Thirty-five percent of the world's mangrove swamps—essential breeding habitat for many marine fish species and recently discovered to be crucial for the survival of coral-reef systems—have already been lost, and the rate of destruction is accelerating annually. Similarly, 15 percent of sea-grass meadows—a shallow coastal feature that helps to limit erosion, recycle nutrients, and provide breeding and feeding grounds for fisheries—have been lost in the last decade.

Surviving ecosystems would be not merely simplified but impoverished to the point where they would fail to provide a range of services we depend on. Coastal wetlands might become too fragile to blunt the storm surge of hurricanes; freshwater wetlands would lose their capacity to filter heavy metals and biological toxins from the effluent of sewage-treatment facilities. Rainforests would lose immense amounts of their pharmacological potential before we even knew what was there.

Benign neglect would fuel an increase in the predominance of pests, parasites, and disease-causing organisms among the weedy species. In the eastern United States coyote populations are already moving into suburban neighborhoods, making cats the meal du jour. In a show of feline solidarity, hungry cougars scan suburbia for dogs (and joggers). Meanwhile, white-tailed deer populations have been allowed to grow virtually unchecked. There are now over 350,000 deer-auto collisions a year in the United States, resulting in over 10,000 serious injuries to motorists, 150 human deaths annually, and billions of dollars in property damage. (In comparison, there have been fewer than 50 confirmed human killings by mountain lions in the United States in the past hundred years.) In Britain there are about 50,000 auto-deer collisions a year, 2,400 human injuries, and 20 deaths. White-tailed deer are, moreover, an essential vector for the highly debilitating Lyme disease, which is spreading rapidly in the eastern United States. Indeed, many human pathogens and diseases are likely to flourish in this environment, easily skipping around the world, as in the recent case of the SARS virus.

Weedy species themselves will face serious threats in this environment, especially from the influx of alien weedy species. The American crow and the blue jay, for example, have already seen their numbers decimated in many areas of the United States by the alien West Nile Virus, which first struck in 1999. North America's once abundant Canadian hemlock (*Tsuga canadensis*) may soon become a relic and then a ghost, owing to the invasion of the woolly adelgid (*Adelges tsuga annand*). Left unchecked, alien species can even work together. In Britain, the gray squirrel (an introduced alien) helped to destroy native red-squirrel populations with a one-two punch. First the gray squirrel spread the Parapox virus, which infected and killed large numbers of red squirrels.

Then the grays finished the job by taking over the red squirrel habitat and filling it through explosive growth.

What we have seen already suggests that the economic toll from the benign neglect of alien weedy species would be globally disastrous. The economic harm caused by the 50,000 non-native invasive plants, animals, and other organisms already in the United States is approaching $140 billion per year. Florida's government alone spends $45 million annually battling invasive species, which cause some $180 million in agricultural damage. The corresponding ecological damage would be inestimable.

Moreover, this approach would mean the demise of a large proportion of the relic species that have particular psychological importance to humanity: elephants, gorillas, whales, owls, hawks, and other charismatic animals. The United Nations Great Apes Survival Project estimates that every one of the great ape species, already having become a relic, is at risk of becoming a ghost within the next 50 years if we simply allow human selection to proceed. From a humanist standpoint the quality of life on Earth would plummet.

6

THE NOTION THAT WE SHOULD SIMPLY let nature take its course is, in a world so thoroughly dominated by humanity, as dangerous as it is self-contradictory. We cannot simply do nothing; neglect will not be benign. Yet there is nothing we can do to avoid the major manifestations of the end of the wild in the centuries ahead; we have accumulated a mountainous extinction debt that makes recovery and restoration—even with herculean efforts—an illusion.

Since we cannot possibly restore relic and ghost species to their former status, nor ever have the knowledge to pick evolutionary winners and losers, we must stop pretending that the haphazard strategy of protecting some relic and ghost species while preserving crippled biodiversity hot spots and natural communities are actions of any lasting ecological value. In short, we must reset our expectations of what is possible to do with the means and time we possess.

So what should we do?

First and foremost we must come to terms with this basic fact: the end of the wild is fundamentally about us, not about this thing we call the environment. It is about our cultural norms, our values, and our priorities. The end of the wild is about how we have chosen to live and how those choices relate to the world around us.

Despite three decades of global environmentalism (and 150 years of conservationist efforts) the person on the street remains oblivious to the fact that he or she is the engine of human selection. To be sure, blaming greedy corporations and crooked politicians is far less discomfiting than looking in the mirror. But the end of the wild is about us. Demanding instant-on appliances, out-of-season vegetables, and ten-mile-per-gallon armored transports to move groceries home means drilling in the Arctic National Wildlife Refuge. Residents and visitors in the American southwest want to motorboat, fish, and water-ski in a desert biome. And so giant reservoirs are built by siphoning off water from once roaring rivers and turning them dry for months at a time. Desert habitats drown while riparian natural communities dessicate. To achieve lawns free of weeds, fruits and vegetables free of defects, and picnics free of mosquitoes we unload millions of tons of toxic chemicals into the soil, water, and air. Weedy species proliferate; others retreat.

This is not just a problem caused by the world's wealthy. Economic globalization is already raising the economic expectations of billions of people in Asia, Africa, and Latin America. Their only way to satisfy these expectations is to exploit local natural resources. The poor and the hungry cannot afford the luxury of worrying about how their two-acre field cut from a tropical rainforest will affect global biodiversity. Governments are understandably reluctant to remove "squatters" from bioreserves for fear of causing massive social unrest. Economists tell us to wait for the Kuznets curve, which does little more than assure us that everyone will lament the end of the wild hundreds of years from now.

Centuries from now, if the planet is to emerge from the cloud of human selection, what must change is us. We as a global society must develop an ecological identity that underscores the connection between how we live and what happens around us. We already recognize the instrumental relationship we have with the wild: it provides us with natural resources. And we are just beginning to understand the genetic linkages. What remains is for us to wake up and see the moral linkages—the realities of shared existence and shared fate.

The task before us is to shift the balance away from human selection and back toward natural selection. To do this we must lessen drastically our ecological footprint on the landscape, and we can only do this if we move away from our anthropocentric view of the world (what can this centipede do for me?). The long-term slowing of the impact of human selection is only possible through action that comes from within us as individuals and that gains hold as society-wide norms. This cannot be imposed from above through laws or other mandatory institutions.

Undoubtedly this ethical transformation will take many centuries. In the meantime we have a moral obligation to take whatever pragmatic steps are available to smooth the edges of human selection.

RESEARCH Second, we must abandon our humanist love affair with the wild, purging considerations such as landscape aesthetics and romanticist isolation and instead applying the cold light of a necropsy to dissect the collapsing processes of natural selection. Function, not form, must be our sole priority. To this end, we must fill the appalling knowledge gap. We need a massive and sustained two-decade global effort, reminiscent of the International Geophysical Year, to systematically and dynamically map the Earth's biota. Only about 20 percent of the Earth's species have been formally described. We need to know what is here, how it lives, what it does, and what is happening to it if we are to prepare for what will be lost. Then we can discover relations within communities. The results are sometimes surprising, as was the recent discovery of genetic links between corals and humans. Then we must move on to the more complex problem of understanding the intricate genetic and functional relationships that tie species together and link them to abiotic processes—especially where forced relics and ghosts are concerned. How might evolutionary pathways and ecological processes be altered?

All this should be geared toward discovering ways to diminish the human-selection effects of human activities. Agriculture, energy extraction, land development, transportation, water use—all should be rethought and rebuilt using this as a first principle.

Undoubtedly this will be expensive. But spending $100 billion over the next decade to fully understand the dimensions of the accelerating biotic contraction on Earth will have infinitely greater significance for humanity than scratching at the surface of Mars for signs of remotely hypothetical billion-year-old bacterial extinctions.

PROTECTING THE LANDSCAPE We must move forward to safeguard future evolutionary processes and pathways and to preserve ecosystem processes and functions. We should concentrate on protecting and preserving still strong and vibrant ecosystems and natural communities and abandon the old approach of trying to save biodiversity piecemeal at its weakest points. Conversely, disturbing healthy ecosystems and natural communities should be undertaken only as a last resort, and then only with the most stringent safeguards against the effects of human selection. But many vestigial relic communities and ghost species must, unfortunately, be allowed to vanish.

Not surprisingly, the heart of this work is in the preservation and protection of huge swaths of landscape and seascape connected across regions and continents. The design of these natural-area trusts, or NATs, is driven, first and foremost, by the need to insulate intact evolutionary processes and healthy ecosystem functions as much as possible from the effects of human selection—admittedly not an easy task given that all surviving ecosystems and habitats are submerged in a far larger ocean of human activity where human selection operates in full force and weedy species proliferate.

Sites would be selected to protect broad ecosystem functions and processes in a dynamic environment rather than species-specific needs (so-called critical habitat). For this reason Yellowstone National Park should be considering what population of bison enriches and strengthens the Yellowstone ecosystem, not how many bison the Yellowstone ecosystem can tolerate. Some NATs would be selected with the realization that their full ecological value lies in the future as the effects of human selection—landscape fragmentation and changes in temperature and precipitation, for example—manifest themselves.

NATs would need highly porous wildlife boundaries within a broad network of corridors and connections (e.g., forest tracts and wetlands), allowing wildlife to move freely and stochastically to new areas. Movement, migration, and colonization are the goals of NATS, not imprisonment. These corridors would be buffered by wide swaths of landscape where ecologically compatible agriculture (e.g., water use) and heavily regulated resource use were allowed. Humans abutting these NATs would need a stewardship mentality, in contrast to that of the herders in Africa who slaughter lions or the cattle grazers in the American west who make war on everything from buffalo to prairie dogs.

Again, the objective is to isolate the effects of human selection, not to isolate human activity. We must discover new ways to do old things.

INTENSIVE MANAGEMENT Ironically, one essential strategy for decoupling the effects of human selection from human activities is more heavy-handed management of the wild. Plant and animal populations within these NATs will have to be actively and heavily managed. This is exactly the opposite of how we think about present-day bioreserves, where intensive manipulation is eschewed. Ironically, natural selection operating in the shadow of human selection will require the active hand of man to emulate natural processes. For example, the remaining populations of Great Basin pika find themselves trapped in higher-elevation sites in the western United States. They are unable to move among potential meta-population sites (to escape human encroachment) because the warming climate has installed a thermal barrier through which they cannot pass. If these creatures are going to survive, we are going to have to physically move them in pattern-mimicking meta-population dynamics.

We may be called upon to determine population levels within the NATs as well as the right time to refresh the genetic foundation of a species, as we are now doing with the Florida panther.

Restricted-range and sessile species would require our explicit intervention to disperse them to potential new habitats. The dwarf cinquefoil (*Potentilla robbinsiana*) is a natural relic found in only two locations in New Hampshire, both endangered by adjacent hiking trails. A cooperative program between the U.S. Fish and Wildlife Service, the Appalachian Mountain Club, and the New England Wildflower Society began breeding these plants in captivity. Mature plants were then reintroduced in new, remote locations in the wild. This process could be carried even further by planting in ecologically linked alpine areas outside historic ranges.

Protecting the integrity and complexity of ecosystem processes and insulating evolutionary pathways from human selection will demand the rigorous enforcement of NAT boundaries. This will cost money: annual global spending on ecosystem protection (including acquisition) is just over $3 billion (the price of two B-2 bombers). Yet obviously it is not enough. For instance, with money to buy out illegal communities and then enforce the borders, the Mexican government might be able to save Montes Azules. We must do a lot better.

Alien plant and animal species must be rigorously managed. A more serious effort to control the flow of exotic parasites, pests, and predators is essential. More-serious attempts to control the flow of alien species will certainly increase the cost of global commerce and disrupt short-term profits. But it will save far more in the costs associated with trying to eradicate destructive alien pests such as the zebra muscle or the Formosan termite.

Finally, we have an obligation to continue prohibitive policies such as the Endangered Species Act and CITES. They buy time in the near term for us to examine the ecological roles of relic and ghost species and assess the impact of their loss on ecosystems. Perhaps they can help us to maintain viable source populations of still-plentiful relics for the next 100 years as we try to put in place larger-scale landscape protection. But these are simple measures with transitory effects; they are not a prescription for restoring nature.

Therefore, we should not evaluate these efforts in terms of their capacity to stop the end of the wild. Their enduring value is that they establish a moral imperative. Like the Ten Commandments, they remind us who we could be. They make us examine our behavior and obligations as the planet's stewards. What is the essence of our own morality if it fails to encompass most of the life on Earth?

7

SINCE THE INVENTION OF THE FIRST stone tool, humanity has pounded the wild into a shape that fits its needs. Forests are transformed to fields. Swamps are drained. Arid landscapes are irrigated. Mountains are flattened and valleys filled. The bounty of nature is converted into commodities: timber, food, luxuries. Coexisting with nature has always meant taming it—consuming it. As the human population jumped into the billions the rise of human selection as the dominant evolutionary force was inevitable, and so was the end of the wild.

Of course, the end of the wild does not mean a barren world. There will continue to be plenty of life covering the globe. There will be birds, mammals, and insects—lots of insects. Life will just be different: much less diverse, much less exotic, much more predictable, and much less able to capture the awe and wonder of the human spirit. Ecosystems will organize around a human motif, the wild will give way to the predictable, the common, the usual. Everyone will enjoy English house sparrows; no one will enjoy wood thrushes.

We have lost the wild for now. Perhaps in five or ten million years it will return.

NOTES

PAGE

4 *a rate of less than one per year*   David S. Woodruff, "Declines of Biomes and Biotas in the Future of Evolution," *Proceedings of the National Academy of Sciences* 98, no. 10 (2001): 5471–5476.

5 *the broad path for evolution is set*   James W. Kirchner and Anne Weil, "Delayed biological recovery from extinctions throughout the fossil record," *Nature* 404 (March 9, 2000): 177–180.

8 *"wilderness"*   U.S. Code, Title 16, Chapter 23, Section 1131 (c).

9 *weedy species*   I borrow this term from David Quammen's seminal "A Planet of Weeds: Tallying the losses of Earth's animals and plants," *Harper's Magazine*, October 1, 1998.

12 *the Nature Conservancy's expedition*   The Nature Conservancy, "Scientists Discover a New Animal and Plant Species Hidden Deep in Bor-

neo Jungles." News release. The Nature Conservancy, http://nature.org/pressroom/press/press1707.html (accessed December 20, 2004).

13 *the African elephant and the giant panda*   Norman Myers and Andrew H. Knoll, "The biotic crisis and the future of evolution," *Proceedings of the National Academy of Sciences* 98, no. 10 (2001): 5389–5392.

15 *the lion population has plunged*   Stephanie Pain, "The Last of the Lions," *New Scientist*, September 20, 2003.

15 *the stocks of large predatory fish*   Ransom A. Myers and Boris Worm, "Rapid Worldwide Depletion of Predatory Fish Communities," *Nature* 423 (May 15, 2003): 280–283.

16 *a vast extinction debt*   Ilkka Hanski and Otso Ovaskinen, "Extinction Debt at Extinction Threshold," *Conservation Biology* 16, no. 3 (2002): 666–673.

17 *weedy species can follow us*   Michael L. McKinney and Julie L. Lockwood, "Biotic Homogenization: A Few Winners Replacing Many Losers in the Next Mass Extinction," *Trends in Ecological Evolution* 14, no. 11 (1999): 450–453.

19 *the causes of the collapse*   For an excellent analysis see the following: Peter Vitousek et al., "Human Domination of Earth's Ecosystems," *Science*

777, no. 25 (1997): 494–499. David Western, "Human-Modified Ecosystems and Future Evolution," *Proceedings of the National Academy of Sciences* 98, no. 10 (2001): 5458–5465.

29 *habitats will become inhospitable*   Gian-Reto Walther et al., "Ecological responses to recent climate change," *Nature* 416 (March 28, 2002): 389–395.

30 *dozens of species of frogs*   J. Allen Pounds et al., "Widespread Amphibian Extinctions from Epidemic Disease Driven by Global Warming," *Nature* 429 (January 12, 2006): 161–167.

30 *climate shift and species survival*   David S. Woodruff, "Declines of Biomes and Biotas in the Future of Evolution," *Proceedings of the National Academy of Sciences* 98, no. 10 (2001): 5472.

31 *the inability to disperse*   Chris D. Thomas et al., "Extinction Risk from Climate Change," *Nature* 427 (January 8, 2004): 145–148.

32 *beef production*   Environmental News Service, "Demand for Brazilian Beef Blamed for Amazon Deforestation," April 6, 2004.

48 *U.S. wildlife refuge system*   Brian Czech, "The Capacity of the National Wildlife Refuge System to Conserve Threatened and Endangered Animal Species in the United States," *Conservation Biology* 19, no. 4 (2005): 1246–1253.

93

48 *the failures of managed bioreserves* John Terbough, *Requiem for Nature* (Washington, D.C.:
Island Press, 1999); John F. Oates, *Myth and Reality in the Rain Forest* (Berkeley, CA: University
of California Press, 1999).

50 *the cloud forest* R.O. Lawton et al., "Climatic
Impact of Tropical Lowland Deforestation on
Nearby Montane Cloud Forests," *Science* 294
(October 19, 2001): 584–587.

52 *the Monarch Butterfly Bioreserve* Karen Ober-
hauser and A. Townsend Peterson, "Modeling
Current and Future Potential Wintering Distri-
butions of Eastern North American Monarch
Butterfly," *Proceedings of the National Academy
Of Sciences* 100, no. 24 (2003): 14063–14068.

53 *transplanting African megafauna* Josh Donlan,
"Rewilding North America," *Nature* 436 (August
18, 2005): 913–914.

56 *Brazil-nut harvest* Carlos Peres et al., "Demo-
graphic Threats to the Sustainability of Brazil Nut
Exploitation," *Science* 302 (2003): 2112–2114.

57 *ecotourism fails the test* Terbough, *Requiem for
Nature.*

66 *keystone species* Yvonne Baskin, *The Work of
Nature* (Washington, D.C.: Island Press, 1997),
15–38.

66 *the invisible hand of the market* In theory,

scarcity, substitution, and the Kuznetz curve should prevent such economic excesses. In reality, multiple market failures make them the rule rather than the exception.

68 *impoverished surviving ecosystems*   Gretchen Daily, ed., *Nature's Services: Societal Dependence on Natural Ecosystems* (Washington, D.C.: Island Press, 1997).

69 *cougars scan suburbia for dogs (and joggers)*   David Baron, *A Beast in the Garden* (W.W. Norton, 2003).

71 *native red squirrel populations in Britain*   D.M. Tompkins, A.R. White, and M. Boots, "Ecological replacement of native red squirrels by invasive greys driven by disease," *Ecology Letters* 6 (2003): 189–196.

71 *Florida's battle against invasive species*   J.R. Pegg, "U.S. Losing War Against Alien Species," *Environmental News Service,* December 19, 2003.

72 *great ape species*   Great Apes Survival Project, *The Great Apes: The Road Ahead,* United Nations Environment Program, http://www.unep.org/grasp/index.asp, 2003.

74 *our choices and the world around us*   Aldo Leopold, *Sand County Almanac* (Ballantine Books, 1986).

76 *the Kuznets curve*   This reflects a theory—

entirely discredited when it comes to protecting natural resources—that postulates that all people develop an environmental conscience once they acquire enough wealth.

77 *ecological identity*   Mitchell Thomashow, *Ecological Identity* (Cambridge, Mass.: MIT Press, 1996).

79 *relations within communities*   Andrew Balmford, Rhys E. Green, and Martin Jenkins, "Measuring the Changing State of Nature," *Trends in Ecology and Evolution* 18, no. 7 (2003): 326–330.

79 *genetic links between corals and humans*   R. D. Kortschak et al., "EST analysis of the cnidarian *Acropora millepora* reveals extensive gene loss and rapid sequence divergence in the model invertebrates," *Current Biology* 13 (2003): 2190–2195.

81 *natural-area trusts*   The root of this idea of huge reserves tied together by "megalinkages" across regions and continents is most seriously developed and promoted by the Wildlands Project. Wildlands Project, *Scientific Overview of the Wildlands Project,* http://www.twp.org, 2005.

85 *Great Basin pika*   Donald Grayson, "A brief history of the Great Basin Pika," *Journal of Biogeography* 32 (2005): 21203–2110.

86 *breeding dwarf cinquefoil in captivity*   William E. Brumback, "An Alpine Implant Comes Back—

Dwarf Cinquefoil," *Endangered Species Bulletin*, U.S. Fish and Wildlife Service, August 2002.

86 *the Mexican government might be able to save Montes Azules*   Marion Lloyd, "Mexico Torn as Threats Rise," *The Boston Globe,* January 25, 2004, sec. A6.

BOSTON REVIEW BOOKS

Boston Review books are accessible, short books that take ideas seriously. They are animated by hope, committed to equality, and convinced that the imagination eludes political categories. The editors aim to establish a public space in which people can loosen the hold of conventional preconceptions and start to reason together across the lines others are so busily drawing.

THE END OF THE WILD   Stephen M. Meyer

GOD AND THE WELFARE STATE   Lew Daly